REACHING FOR THE STARS

LUKE PERRY

by: Rosemary Wallner

Published by Abdo & Daughters, 6535 Cecilia Circle, Edina, Minnesota 55439.

Library bound edition distributed by Rockbottom Books, Pentagon Tower, P.O. Box 36036, Minneapolis, Minnesota 55435.

Printed in the United States.

Cover Photo: Shooting Star
Inside Photos: Shooting Star 4, 12, 17, 19, 22 & 31
                 Out-line Press Syndicate Inc. 25 & 27
                 Archive Photo 6, 9 & 14

Edited by Bob Italia

LIBRARY OF CONGRESS CATALOGING-IN-PUBLICATION DATA

Wallner, Rosemary. 1964-
    Luke Perry / written by Rosemary Wallner.
        p. cm. — (Reaching for the Stars)
    Summary: Examines the life and career of one of the popular stars of the television show "Beverly Hills 90210."
    ISBN 1-56239-146-1
    1. Perry, Luke -- Juvenile literature. 2. Television actors and actresses -- United States -- Biography -- Juvenile literature. [1. Perry, Luke. 2. Actors and actresses.] I. Title. II. Series.
PN2287.P395W35 1992   791.45'028'092--dc20   92-16036
                                          [B]

International Standard Book Number:	Library of Congress Catalog Card Number:
1-56239-146-1	92-16036

TABLE OF CONTENTS

Cast of the hit show, Beverly Hills, 90210.

4

FROM NO NAME TO SUPERSTAR

The Fox-TV series "Beverly Hills, 90210" has thousands of loyal viewers. The show's fans love the clothes, the cars, and the talented actors and actresses. Shannen Doherty, who plays Brenda Walsh, and Jason Priestley, who plays Brandon Walsh, were stars from the show's start. Other characters didn't catch viewers' eyes right away. Fans needed time to get to know Ian Ziering (Steve Sanders), Jennie Garth (Kelly Taylor), and Luke Perry (Dylan McKay).

But Luke isn't complaining. He has become one of the show's most popular stars. His character is mysterious. He is a guy with a dark past who has fallen for Brenda.

Luke admits his character is smooth. Dylan knows what to say and he takes his time saying it. "He's the type of guy I would want as a friend," said Luke. "He's independent and intelligent—a free spirit. I like that. Dylan has a sense of what's right and wrong."

Luke Perry

GROWING UP IN OHIO

Coy Luther Perry III was born on October 11, 1966, in Mansfield, Ohio. He grew up in the nearby farming community of Fredericktown. Luke has an older brother Tom and a younger sister Amy.

Ever since he was four years old, Luke wanted to be an actor. "I've always been a big fan of television and movies," he explained. All he ever wanted to do was act on TV or on the big screen.

When Luke was six years old, his parents Ann and Coy, Sr., divorced. Luke never talked to his father after that. When his father died eight years later, Luke went to his funeral. He admitted, though, that he and his father were never close.

For six years after the divorce, Mrs. Perry raised her children by herself. When Luke was twelve years old, his mother remarried. Luke liked his stepfather, Steve Bennett. Steve was a construction worker who had a daughter Emily from a previous marriage. He took Luke and his brother to work with him on weekends. The two brothers learned much about the construction business.

"He's the greatest man I know," said Luke about his stepfather. "I love him. He's the one who taught me the important things I needed to know about being a man."

As a teenager, Luke attended Fredericktown High School. His school was in a farming community. Luke's classes were different from those in large cities. "We had classes on giving birth to cows and driving tractors," he remembered. In school, Luke liked history and science; he admitted that he never did like math.

Luke was popular in high school. His friends knew him as a caring and loyal pal. Luke remains close to many of his high school friends. "The best friends of my life come from that small town," Luke said. "Some of the best people who I know are there. I call them all the time."

Luke played baseball and tennis for Fredericktown. He was also the school's mascot, which the students called the "Freddie Bird." For one football game, Luke rented a helicopter from his stepfather's company. The copter airlifted him onto the field. When it landed, Luke jumped out wearing his costume—yellow tights, red plumes, a cape, and giant webbed feet.

*Luke Perry with Brian Austin Green, during a
celebrity baseball game.*

Luke had a wild side in high school, too. He admitted getting into trouble once in awhile. Luke's hometown was small and he became frustrated when he couldn't pursue acting. His school had no drama classes. His town had no community theater. It didn't even have a movie theater. To vent his frustration, Luke acted wild. He rode his dirt bike around the track at games, doing wheelies. He cut classes. He argued with the principal. At the time he thought he knew more than his teachers.

Luke also had many girlfriends in high school. In his senior year, his class voted him the "Biggest Flirt." Right before his senior prom, Luke found that he had two different dates ("I don't know how that happened!" he said). But it all worked out in the end. Luke took the girl he had asked first.

HEADING TO CALIFORNIA

In 1985, Luke graduated from high school. Now he could finally pursue his dream of acting. He and a friend packed up a small car and drove two thousand miles to Los Angles, California.

"I moved to Hollywood to get warm because I was sick of freezing in Ohio during the winter!" joked Luke. "Once I got here, I thought, 'Well, acting is really the reason why I'm here. Come on, let's get going!'"

The two Ohioans found an apartment in Orange County near Los Angeles. Luke enrolled in acting classes and found small parts at the local Whitefire Theater in Sherman Oaks. He met David Beard, who became his acting coach. When his friend moved back to Ohio, Luke moved to Hollywood by himself.

Bobby Hoffman, an agent, encouraged Luke. He told the young actor that he had real potential. Bobby told Luke to keep trying, something would come his way. As he waited for auditions, Luke earned money doing odd jobs. He flipped hamburgers, sold shoes, and worked in a doorknob factory. He also worked at construction sites and on road crews. One of his jobs was to paint lines in the Torrance High School parking lot. Although he didn't know it at the time, that school would become the set for *Beverly Hills, 90210*.

Luke Perry as a soap opera star.

12

Luke went on hundreds of auditions. He tried out for commercials, radio voice-overs, TV shows, and small parts in movies. In 1987, after three years of trying, Luke became discouraged. Then he heard about a producer in New York who was casting parts for an afternoon TV soap opera. Luke flew to New York and read for the part. There, he met future 90210er Ian Ziering, who was also trying out for the part. (Neither Luke nor Ian got the part.)

Luke didn't give up. He tried out for another soap opera. On his 217th audition, he landed the role of Ned Bates on the ABC soap opera *Loving*.

THE LIFE OF A SOAP OPERA ACTOR

Getting the part on *Loving* meant Luke had to move to New York. At first he was hesitant about living in the huge city, but he learned to love it. He found an apartment in the Upper West side and began his acting career.

Luke described his soap opera character as a sweet country boy from Tennessee. "I've been involved in several fights (as Ned)," he said at the time.

Luke admits he wants to do stunt work.

14

"America calls Ned the wimp! (He's) been beaten up three times by five people!"

Luke began to take acting seriously. He watched other actors. He learned how to improve himself. He also learned to memorize many pages of script and prepare himself for the daily shootings. "On the soaps, I'd have to memorize twenty pages of dia- logue a night, which is a lot to remember!" he said.

The show *Loving* shared studio space with another ABC soap, *Ryan's Hope*. On the set, Luke met Yasmine Bleeth, who played Ryan Fenelli. The two began spending time together.

Luke spent a year on *Loving*. Although he played only a minor character, he took every opportunity to meet the public. He attended celebrity functions. He signed autographs. He said yes to every publicity offer. He kept running into Ian Ziering, who was also acting in soaps. The two met at various soap events and played softball together.

At the same time, Luke took stunt lessons. "There are more exciting things out there that I want to do," he said at the time. "I want to do stunt work."

After a year, his contract on *Loving* ran out. The producers took Ned Bates off the show. According to Luke, his last scene as Ned Bates was uneventful. In the scene, Luke's character went upstairs to wash his hands. That was the last anyone saw of Ned.

Once again, Luke was unemployed. He went to more auditions. NBC-TV cast him as Kenny on *Another World*, another soap opera. Luke worked on that soap on and off for six months. Then he modeled for a blue jeans ad. The job disappointed him, though, because he couldn't keep any of the jeans. Luke even tried out for a part on the NBC show *Ferris Bueller* with no success.

He had small parts in the movies *Terminal Bliss* and *Scorchers*. In *Scorchers*, he played Ray Ray LaPugh. His character was a crazy, dirty, drunk trapper. Luke admitted that he loved the role.

Despite his best efforts, Luke didn't get any more good acting roles. He decided to move back to Hollywood. He thought his chances for finding jobs were better out west. He was right.

Two months after he returned to the West Coast, his agent told him about a new Fox-TV show, *Class of Beverly Hills*.

The cast of Beverly Hills, 90210.

THE 90210 AUDITION

In the early spring of 1990, Fox-TV began an open casting call for *Class of Beverly Hills*. Anyone who wanted a part on the new show could audition. The studio saw thousands of young people. They were all eager to portray high school teenagers.

Luke's agent called Luke at his construction job and told him he had an audition with the show's casting board. Luke had to tell his boss huge lies to get out of work that day. When his boss finally said he could go, Luke had another obstacle. He needed something to wear. That day he hadn't worn a shirt to work. He grabbed an old shirt out of a friend's car trunk. The shirt had oil spots and lacked buttons. Luke tied it on and headed for the audition.

Once at the studio, he waited for his turn in a little room with James Eckhouse, who was auditioning for the part of Mr. Walsh. Both actors were nervous but tried to keep themselves under control. Luke, however, couldn't overcome his nervousness. He ran to the bathroom and threw up.

*(L to R) Jason Priestly, Carol Potter, James Eckhouse and
Shannon Doherty.*

19

At first, Luke auditioned for the part of Steve Sanders, which eventually went to his friend Ian Ziering. The producers thought Luke might be the right actor to play Dylan McKay.

"When Luke walked into the audition, it was like 'Wow, that's the person,' " said the show's creator Darren Star. Luke knew he wanted the part when he picked up the audition script. Luke kept repeating to himself, "Oh, man, they got to take me! They got to, they got to!"

Dylan was the last role created for the show. The writers originally wrote him in for only one episode. In fact, the character didn't even appear in the pilot (first) episode. "After the pilot, we felt there should be someone who is a little dangerous, a little on the edge," said producer Aaron Spelling. "And we came up with the Dylan character." The producer made other changes to the show. He decided to use the area's zip code in the title so he changed the series name from *Class of Beverly Hills* to *Beverly Hills, 90210.*

After the third casting call, the producers told Luke he had the part. Getting the job meant many changes in Luke's life.

He knew that his move to California was permanent; and that meant leaving Yasmine Bleeth. According to Luke, the two decided to end their relationship.

Luke's character appeared in the first show of 1991, which was titled "Isn't It Romantic?" Luke played the character so well, the writers added him to the main cast.

THOUGHTS ON DYLAN AND THE CAST

When asked what he likes best about his *90210* character, Luke's reply is simple. "One of the great things about Dylan is that he shows that it's cool to be smart," said Luke. "He's an intellectual and kind of a loner. Dylan doesn't care about fitting in. That's why we're very similar. Nobody knows where I fit in, least of all me!"

Luke knows that Dylan has his softer side. Although the character seems to know what he's doing, sometimes he's not sure at all.

Luke likes the intellectual side of the character "Dylan".

In that way, Luke is like Dylan. As Luke said, "I don't pretend that I have it all together and I don't pretend that I know everything. I don't."

There is another similarity between the actor and his character. Both like to stand back, watch things, and remain detached. Both don't jump into a situation right away.

For a show to be a success, it needs more than just great actors. The behind-the-scenes people can really make a difference. Luke is quick to point out the crew's long hours. Many jobs are on the line. The pressure on Luke and the other cast members to succeed is intense.

The writers are a behind-the-scenes group Luke admires. The *90210* writers have shown many different sides of his character, Luke said. They have changed Dylan since his first episode and made him more vulnerable. He still keeps up a cool front, though. Dylan isn't ready for his friends to see every side of him.

When Luke thinks there is a problem, he sometimes talks about it with Chuck Rosin, the executive producer. Luke describes what he thinks should happen.

Chuck usually counters with another idea. Together, they reach compromises. Although Luke doesn't always get his way, he's glad the producers and writers listen to him.

According to Luke, the whole *90210* cast is fun. All the cast members, he added, work hard. When the show became more popular, the cast could hardly believe it. Their success made them work harder to create an even better show.

Working every day with the same people can get hard sometimes. "There are some days that people don't get along as well as others," admitted Luke. But the bad moods never seem to last long. "It's not always easy," added Luke, "but I wouldn't trade these guys for anything."

On the set, Luke's good friends include Jason Priestley and Ian Ziering. All three live away from their families. (Jason is from Vancouver, Canada, and Ian is from New Jersey.) The three actors turn to each other for support.

Just as in his soap opera days, Luke continues to meet his fans. Since *90210,* he has traveled around the country on promotional tours.

Luke Perry's close friends, Jason Priestly and Shannon Doherty.

He rarely turns down interviews. He poses for pictures and appears on talk shows.

Between rehearsals and interviews, Luke strives to improve himself as an actor. "I have to be critical of my performance," he said. "It's the only way I can improve." So far, he's proud of the work he has done and he's happy with the series.

"Other shows about teenagers are either too preachy or put on a candy-coated view of life," he said. "*Beverly Hills, 90210* isn't preachy. And we're certainly not candy-coated!"

LUKE PERRY IN PRIVATE

Thousands of people see Luke every week on *90210*. But many of his fans wonder about the real Luke Perry. One thing his fans may not know is that the actor is shy. Luke still gets nervous whenever he has to face a crowd.

Luke doesn't get nervous, though, when he bungee jumps. (In bungee jumping, a person jumps off a bridge or high crane while attached to an elastic bungee cord.)

Luke Perry thrives on excitement.

He usually jumps with his pal Jason Priestley, who first told Luke about the sport. "I like constant excitement in my life," said Luke. "I like the challenge of doing things that scare me." Luke added that this daredevil sport is the most exciting thing he has ever done.

Luke also likes tamer pastimes. He can often be found on the basketball court playing a game with friends. He also enjoys fishing, good movies, and listening to classic rock and roll and opera. His favorite musicians are B. B. King and Jerry Lee Lewis. He even named his pet Chinese potbellied pig Jerry Lee.

Since the studio cast him on *90210,* Luke has lived in the Los Angeles area—far away from his family and friends. "It's difficult for my family to see each other often," said Luke. "I live in Hollywood, Tom is in Chicago, and everyone else is in Ohio. But we sure try."

Has Luke changed much since his rise to stardom? Luke admitted that, at first, he liked all the attention. But he didn't want to get carried away with it. He told himself that if the Hollywood lifestyle ever started to change him, he would leave. "I'd go back to Ohio and get a job driving an ambulance," he said.

He doesn't think about being famous anymore. "That's not my job, being famous," he said. "My job is to act."

SERIOUS ABOUT ACTING

Luke takes his job on *90210* seriously. After each workday, he heads home to study his script. He has vowed not to do anything halfway. "I feel I have to give just as much as everyone else," Luke said. "This show is a team effort, from the actors to the technicians to the people who copy the script."

Luke also likes to keep active in his community. He is a spokesperson for "Traffic Safety Now." The group supports wearing seat belts while riding in a car. Luke became involved in the cause because some of his high school friends who were not wearing seat belts died in a car accident.

He also supports Greenpeace, a group determined to preserve all aspects of the environment. "Wake up to what's going on in the environment," said Luke. "Start recycling. Be prepared and don't close your eyes to the problems of the world."

To help children with AIDS, Luke played basketball for MTV's Rock 'N' Jock Basketball Jam in Los Angeles. All the proceeds went to the Pediatric AIDS Foundation.

With lines to study and functions to attend, Luke hardly has time to answer his fan mail. Each week Luke and Jason receive 1,500 letters. "I love getting fan mail," beamed Luke. "It's difficult to answer it all but I'm going to try."

Luke enjoys meeting his fans and is glad that they want to see him. He gets upset, though, when fans get out of control. That is one reason he enjoys doing things with Jason and Ian. If the three get recognized, Luke said, at least there is safety in numbers.

Since he takes his acting seriously, there seems to be nothing Luke can't do. He has signed a two-picture movie deal with Twentieth Century Fox studios. In April 1992, Luke's first film was rumored to be about a rodeo star. Any movies he does make, however, will be done when *90210* is on break.

Luke Perry, takes his acting seriously.

Will Luke ever leave *Beverly Hills, 90210* ? That's not likely. "I'll stay as long as they'll have me!" Luke said. "I really love it, and I'll stay on the show as long as they tell me to keep coming back."

LUKE PERRY'S ADDRESS

You can write to Luke Perry at:

Luke Perry
Beverly Hills, 90210
Fox-TV
10201 W. Pico Boulevard
Los Angeles, CA 90035

If you want to receive a reply, enclose a self-addressed stamped envelope.